Welcome To
I SPY
HALLOWEEN

This book belongs to :

....

I spy with my little eye something beginning with...

I spy with my little eye something beginning with...

B is for

Bat

I spy with my little eye something beginning with...

C is for

Candle

I spy with my little eye something beginning with...

D

E is for Eyeball

F is for Frankenstein

I spy with my little eye something beginning with...

G is for

Ghost

I spy with my little eye something beginning with...

H is for Hat

I spy with my little eye something beginning with...

I is for

Ice Cream

J is for

Jack-o'-lantern

I spy with my little eye something beginning with...

K and L†

K is for King

L is for Lantern

I spy with my little eye something beginning with...

M is for Mummy

I spy with my little eye something beginning with...

O and P

O is for

Owl

P is for

Pumpkin

I spy with my little eye something beginning with...

Q is for

Queen

I spy with my little eye something beginning with...

R is for Raven

I spy with my little eye something beginning with...

S

and

T

S is for

Skeleton

T is for

Turkey

U is for Unicorn

V is for Vampire

I spy with my little eye something beginning with...

W is for Witch

I spy with my little eye something beginning with...

X is for

X-Ray

Y is for

Yarn

I spy with my little eye something beginning with...

Made in the USA
Middletown, DE
15 August 2022